# DISSENT

DISSENT
Copyright © 2025 Kathleen Nalley and Gabrielle Brant Freeman

For permissions and information on ordering books, contact operations@smallharborpublishing.com.

Cover art: Gabrielle Brant Freeman, "Eleutheria"
Editor: Jessie Truong
Publisher: Allison Blevins
Director: Kristiane Weeks-Rogers
Managing Editor: Bianca Dagostino

DISSENT
Kathleen Nalley and Gabrielle Brant Freeman
ISBN 978-1-957248-60-8
Harbor Editions,
an imprint of Small Harbor Publishing

# DISSENT

## Kathleen Nalley and Gabrielle Brant Freeman

Harbor Editions
Small Harbor Publishing

This collection is dedicated to the single mother, the traumatized daughter, the ones living paycheck to paycheck, those without vacation, the burnt out, the underpaid, the overworked, the silent, the scared, the anxious, the invisible, the dismissed, the disappeared.

To the Kathleen and Gabrielle who met 15 years ago on a wood porch on the side of a mountain, blood under our nails, and the women we have become, blood in our teeth.

To you, in this moment. Say it with us.

# Contents

# DISSENT

## About This Collection

Two friends embarked on a 35-day writing quest: to each write a sonnet per day in response to and/or inspired by the previous, lifting a word, phrase, or idea for use in the subsequent poem, ultimately creating a sinuous, echoing, loose sonnet sequence that examines thoughts leading up to Inauguration Day, January 20, 2025.

## 12/16/24
## Bitter

I just want an afternoon alone, a scarred
surface, pasta al dente tossed with butter,
minced garlic, delicate parmesan, zest
of a lemon, ripe potential, cruel fruit

of this tree I just bought. Petals unfurl
a promise, a premise, fruit thick, dimpled,
my thighs in no hurry to hide their pith
and rind. Split the yellow leather skin

to citric sections with a sharp steel blade.
I am in no mood to be dissected.
Lemon bite stings my gums. I wear its wedge
in a maniacal smile. I am split.

My mouth waters with anger, bright and cruel.
He said, *You'd be prettier if you smiled.*

12/16/24
Perimenopause


My mouth waters with anger, bright and cruel,
sour-tinged taste on the just-loosened tongue.
I quake awake from another nightmare, clenched,
hard bite and mandible heavy, the constant dull

thrum in my left temple. If only I
had hammer, machete, icepick, pitchforks
to javelin into targets. I am
all body, chin hair, crow-ridden, large scar.

Morning hips ache as if readying for
the down, death, drone attack, hidden battle.
Every day is some fresh hell, the body
on the brink of something big, maybe war.

Before the last egg descends, like Goya's
Saturn, I want to devour them all.

12/17/24
Your Body, My Choice

This is the face that greets you, madness slashed,
lidless eyes wide over the black rack of mouth,
the pale body pinioned in his pinched grip,
bloody stump of neck, pendulous hips,

the body on the brink of something big,
maybe war. I imagine Goya painting
this scene by his window, private horror,
a man caught in the act but still eating,

offensive tumescence removed for viewing.
But look! You can see it there, right? Erect
between the gnarly knees? Historians
named it *Saturn Devouring His Son*, but

full buttocks, sensuous shoulders, shock of skin?
Women will revolve. Cut our tortured teeth.

12/17/24
Imprint


On my left leg a tattoo of Venus
rises out of books instead of a clam.
On my right leg, blank canvas. You warned me
against tattooing the 2008


"Medusa with the Head of Perseus"
into my calf because it rewrites myth.
Isn't it enough that she can turn men
to stone? Render them toothless? Take away


their ability to move, to maim, to
monster? In the statue, Medusa's made
beautiful—tamed hair, muscular, undoomed,
full buttocks, sensuous shoulders, shock of skin—


Maybe historians misread Goya.
Men tend to believe whatever they're told.

12/18/24
#tradwife


No milkmaid dress, no cowboy boots, no face
framed in salon waves; in postwar rural
Minnesota, my grandmother mucked
the chicken coop, broke necks, scalded, plucked,

gutted hens to feed her husband, a farmer
kept home to grow corn, soybeans, to toil
in fields for the greater good. My grandfather
whose left hand was maimed, whose black hair was shorn,

whose mom was forced to a reservation
far from her traditional home. Isn't it
funny how people think history fixed
even though the veneer clearly peels

revealing the monster? High maintenance
propaganda. Prosthetic and white.

12/19/24
Revealing

When Titus Kaphar portrays Jefferson—
adorned in white cambric stock, black waistcoat,
stoic sliver of lip, barely blushed skin—
the painted canvas peels away, exposes

an unadorned, naked Sally Hemmings
wearing only a teal and gold headscarf,
her body, cleverly hidden behind
the folds of canvas with Jefferson's face.

Often, people think history something
to go back to, to be celebrated—
founding fathers, all prosthetic and white,
women, silent, submissive, subservient.

But remember: cornered things fight or fly.
Women in kitchens concoct alchemy.

12/19/24
Abscess


When I was young, I believed the gentle folds
of foothills, the craggy spans of mountains
cleverly hid sleeping giants. Slumber
so deep that forests unfurled over them.

Moss, rocks shot out when they rolled in their beds,
chased their giant dreams of gold, of bone bread.
When they woke, they would wear the scrim of soil
like coats, pine spikes adorning their shoulders.

How was I to know, a girl blanketed
in wonder, that giants do not sleep.
They mine and they hoard, they flay mountain flesh,
and they eat, Earth oozing between diseased teeth.

Pustules of corruption, an infection of men.
Our planet abrades her hoary skin. She slides.

12/20/24
Plunder

It is said that when Vikings invaded
Benedictine Abbey at Coldingham,
Saint Æbbe razored off her nose, cut off
her upper lip, chiseled her face grotesque,

self-mutilation as preservation
against the threats of men. The other nuns
followed suit, a congress of flailed flesh—
gnarled, gangly faces, such a turn-off,

such a disappointing turn of events.
The Vikings mined and flayed and ate everything
but not the women—they set them ablaze—
this scene, the origin of the saying

cutting off the nose to spite the face, or,
when denied, giants will resort to fire.

12/21/24
## A Woman's Heart

One year after Mary Shelley's death,
the remains of her husband's charred heart
were found wrapped in silk in her desk drawer.
I find myself almost disappointed

at this turn of events. This prophetess
who wrote the man so feminine-jealous
that he razored off charnel parts, stitched them
back, just to prove he, too, could create life

which he then, naturally, abandoned.
There is no applause in the day-to-day work
of raising children, assuming you survive
their birth. I can only hope she kept it

as one would a specimen, examined
in wonder: this heart, too, was woman-made.

12/21/24
Erased


Mary Shelley never knew her mother
in physical form—Mary Wollstonecraft
died after childbirth from sepsis after
the placenta, breaking, became infected.


After her death, Mary's husband published
*Memoirs of the Author of a*
*Vindication of the Rights of Women,*
by William Godwin, Wollstonecraft's name


omitted from the story of her life.
Hughes published Plath's *Ariel* after she
passed, editing her words and structures
and sequences to suit his own ego.


Men, so feminine-jealous, riding on
the skirt hems of the women who loved them.

12/22/24
Bully


Bully used to mean sweetheart, did you know?
But after an editing of structures
and sequences, meaning slunk undercover
into lover, into ruffian, into

a person who eats at another's table,
a jaeger, a thief of a bird which will
chase other species, harass them until
they drop or vomit prey meant for their young,

scoop it up and feast. Someone I once called
sweetheart, a huntsman, a husband, a hanger-
on, made a practice of gaslighting,
erudite parasite, of spinning language

to wool meant to blind me to the violence
of hijacking a life. This is my story.

## 12/23/24
## You Gotta Have Faith

How to hijack a country: put white men
in positions of power, grant them the
legislative strong-arm, stocks and money,
henchmen who will do their bidding, whether

unaliving a threat or paying a 17-year-old
for sex, pretend they have a mandate to
do anything they want because who will
stop them? They could stand in the middle of

Fifth Avenue and shoot somebody; they
could evade taxes, lie, steal, share secrets,
snort coke, grab women by the pussy while
flaunting their faith, declaring the gospel.

Such a pathetic public fantasy.
Such a flaccid phallic fallacy.

12/25/24
Fantasy or Fallacy?


In 1983, I boarded a bus
outside the 7-11. An hour
later, I sat in a class where they told me
what I would learn that year in order to earn

my way into college and a much better
life than my parents, blue-collar workers,
one loading bags on planes, thousands of pounds
a day, the other sorting sentiment,

categorizing cards with Garfield
or Care Bears, greetings for all American
occasions. I envisioned a checkbook
without careful weekly computations,

an unlimited supply of wealth-induced
calm built on brains, not the skin of my teeth.

12/25/24
Sorting Sentiments


New York City woke up to a white
Christmas this morning, big flakes falling
from an extraterrestrial skyline,
underfoot trenches piled with dirty snow.


Lately I've been wringing the worth out of
everything—six potatoes became three
dinners—mashed, potato skins, baked with cheese.
The oranges I candied became


cheesecake decor and simple syrup in a
Mistletoe Manhattan for a cocktail
contest. My hubby makes edibles to
get through another day, and another...


Another school shooting. Another
immolation. All-American occasions.

12/26/24
*Gott Mit Uns*
(God is with Us)


In the classroom, opposing trenches are dug
out of desks over dirty linoleum.
Students lob balled up paper like so much
city snow piling up underfoot.

They will remember the First World War meant
excavation, meant gash in the earth,
meant crowding, meant impacting, meant gas
sinking below the lip of blood soaked dirt.

They will be able to answer correctly
the multiple-choice questions on the test,
and someday they will say, *we are in
the trenches*, and they will mean, *this is hard*.

Consider this brass matchbox, crafted in the cut
from a dead man's belt buckle. This is a test.

12/27/24
Priorities

While fighting for surrender or stalemate,
soldiers prioritized guns over gums—
trench mouth—acute necrotizing ulcerative
gingivitis—rotted whole mouths.

My friend, veteran of Afghanistan,
twelve scars from being stabbed in close combat,
chugs brown liquor every night to dull the
synapses that spark like artillery

fire, his teeth, slowly rotting from the lack
of care, the quieting of the brain
prioritized over those of the mouth,
which can still function even if dying.

He wears a silver belt buckle and his
dog tags just in case. This, too, is a test.

12/28/24
*Wanderwort*


Silver, a word spread through established
trade routes, Bronze Age argonauts, swift sailors
searching for precious cargo, argentum,
*to shine white* like synapses, like branches
in winter knitting sylvan. A migrant word
well-traveled like sugar, like ginger,
like wine and spice everyone everywhere
wanted and needed to name. An amalgam
of language, of culture, a loan word
surrendered through networks of people
just trying to make it make sense,
an emollient evolved to soften,

toxic kintsugi, quicksilver fillings.
We have forgotten our origin story.

12/29/24
HGTV Can Go to Hell


Could it be we're now in the Plastic Age?
Where we've symbolically replaced that which
was once metallic and shining? We are
without luster, imagination—sequel.

Did we forget where we started? Decayed
dinosaurs became oil; extracted oil
becomes plastic; once ingested, plastic
becomes us—synthetic sediment.

Artificial intelligence, fake news,
online persona through filter glow, haze,
nourishment from boxes, powder mixes,
replicated, repeated, disposable.

Reality television scripted.
Destiny already predetermined.

12/29/24
It's Fantastic!

Trash day after Christmas, Any Street,
America. Plastic bins crowned in waste,
wrapping and ribbon, resources used once
to entice—shiny, bright, and new. Next.

Synthetic trees set up and surrounded
with the sediment of consumption.
So many *I didn't know what to get you*'s,
nondescript novelty items packaged

and placed at the checkout, purchased
on impulse, last-minute gifts for those
last on the list. The sheer loss of it all.
We cannot sustain this celebration.

O Christmas tree, O Christmas tree!
I fear our dark machinery.

12/30/24
Artificial Intelligence


I've never forgotten the image of
masked uniformed schoolchildren, in formation,
marching straight into a meat grinder in
Pink Floyd's *The Wall* in the 1980s.


Teacher's paddle, father's belt—most acquiesce
to brute force if delivered long enough
and most brutally. Emerson wrote, *A*
*foolish consistency is the hobgoblin*


*of little minds.* Our blind adherence to
tradition, concentric circles of
repeated patterns spiraling us down.
We're no longer just the cogs; we are the


dark machine itself, dazed, glazed, and fried,
the collateral damage of progress.

12/30/24
## My Donut Soul

I am thinking of Krispy Kreme,
of mechanical donut dispensers
dropping down perfect rows of O-
shaped dough left to rise and then fried,

of paper hats and children watching
donuts sprayed with glaze, popped out and boxed
to go, dozens and dozens a day,
sugar-rush happy Saturday mornings.

I type *write a sonnet about a donut*
into artificial intelligence
and, as though sensing my intent,
it spits this line, *I'm just a snack, man!*

Dazed, glazed, and fried. I bite down into
nothing special. I lick my fingers clean.

12/30/24
First

Aimee from Amarillo and I—bored
latchkey kids with nothing better to do,
both just beginning to blossom—swiped
my older sister's copy of *Forever*

by Judy Blume and, quite literally,
hid in the closet behind louvered doors
reading the juicy parts out loud. Aimee
role-played Michael, timbre-ing her voice,

lengthening her fingers, sliding her hands.
I played Katherine awakening to her
body, its bend and hip, undulating
topography, its lakes and dark caverns.

Spontaneous rows of O's—seismic
shift, gravitational pull in, then out.

12/31/24
Strange Beast

1979, Southern California.
My brother and I slip in from summer
sprinklers and swim practice, prepubescent
rounded bodies wrapped in navy Lycra,
blonde hair greening and heavy with the scent
of chlorine. We flop to the floor, forest
shag, dig in for Godzilla movies,
black and white marathons of monsters
stomping on cities, releasing their rage,
sweeping seismic chaos, like a bomb.
Origin story, indiscriminate
nuclear massacre given form.

All we knew then was to brace for the random
attack, our father's furious footsteps at the door.

12/31/24
Surviving Fallout

After 60 days of no bleeding,
for the first time in 41 years (minus
two pregnancy stints), the blush came rushing
back with a vengeance, red tsunami

between my thighs, on the beige cotton sheets,
my legs and back and abdomen aching,
muscles stretched apart, contracting, widening
hips, all over again, where they'd receded.

How many catastrophes occur in
a woman's body during her lifetime—
detonated bomb, massacre marathon.
Phallopians 4:13: I can do

all things through blood that wrecks me; I can do
fuck all you can do while furiously bleeding.

1/1/25
Realignment

Regrow bone, muscle, cartilage, fat. Multipotent
stem cells are present in each and every
endometrial sloughing, nothing to do
but collect it, but. We have been taught:

Dirty, disgusting, toughen yourself,
hide it, don't cry about it, resign
yourself to the pain, it's not a big deal,
every woman goes through it, seven whole years

of uterine lining renewal. Wait,
don't say uterus, ovulate, menstruate,
can I borrow a tampon, don't say tampon.
Don't let anyone know you're expelling

the most readily available, naturally
occurring, healing fluid known to woman.

1/1/25
New Year, New Outlook

Neither venom nor strychnine this seepage
but nectar, elixir, healing cellular
miracle, the secret of great secrets,
this life secretion, sinuous crimson
potion, God substance, maternal concoction,
potent plague killer, mystic medicine,
living liquid, real blood covenant,
birth portender, life extender, monthly
moon goodness, feminine deity sauce,
magical mystery, alchemical
understatement, misunderstood, discarded,
vilified, maligned, monstered, made nasty.

They incinerate placentas after birth.
They burned us at the stake just for being.

1/3/25
Ignition


Outside the Rack & Snack, I cup last light

in my hands, butane flame sculpting sinuous

curves and planes of my teenaged face, my mom's

magnum opus mirrored in the rearview.

Inside, everyone else uses angle

and force, friction and geometric

decisions to spin phenolic resin spheres

off rails into pockets, rocket and

ricochet this short summer night away.

It is dark, here, by the lake.

Its flat black eye commands, casts a mountain

cracked by asphalt braced in metal, manmade

pact to the Pacific. I promise God

I'll be good if He just lets me bleed.

1/3/25
## The Beautiful Ones

Teenage me dreamed of a fast, Prince-purple
5-speed Corvette, T-tops and pink satin
waterbed seats (don't ask), hanging cherry
air freshener popping from the rearview,
imagined the boys lined up to witness
its rev and spark, its gear-toothed growl, hungry
motors humming, its sinuous curves and
planes mirroring their primal? hormonal?
need to take control, grasp the gearshift with
their greedy hands, ricochet and rocket
from first to second to third in slipping
seconds, to forget that this car was mine.

My first, in college, a used Celica.
Before that, someone else in the driver's seat.

1/3/25
## Dating After Divorce

The angle between the direction
your tires are pointing and the actual
direction of travel is the slip,
grip on the wheel in the curve,
a moment of float, of unknown,
then friction, a glide, a slide into place.

Slip of the lip, sibilant fricative,
he touched tongue to palate, created
constriction, blew past it, gained traction,
such turbulent noise.
*Shut up!* he said.
His intensity got my attention.

Still learning, I thought. At this age.
I went into the turn at full speed.

1/3/25
## Marrying After Dating After Divorce (Again)

Somehow I ended up with a man who
favors fricatives, indicative of
sounds softly squeezing through the teeth: squish, squash,
mash, maize, seize, slice, sling, slope, sloth, slang, slick, slung,

slunk. He also speaks monosyllabically—
impact being of impor:—sharp but blunt,
his ability to cut to the chase.
If we argue, he gruffs but never yells.

When we disagree, he lets it go, never
harbors a grudge, never burdens me with
fear of backdraft when the ember smolders.
I'm his opposite; sometimes I yell, curse.

My favorite word? Fuck—first fricative, then
explosive plosive, hard tack of the K.

1/4/25
## Only the Names are Changed

There is a bridge, but look, it is crumbling.
It is, after all, built of eggshells, broken
down nearly to dust from the tiptoeing.
And of course there's a troll, this one's bespoke,
included because a troll is expected
beneath such a bridge, demanding his due.
His nest is a mess of discards, neglected,
sutured together, thrown on each time his cue
is called. Trip, trap. Shells crack. Masked, he appears.
Poor lost Red sees a prince where stands a thief.
He will sneer, "I told you what my eyes and ears
are for" just before he bares his teeth.

The smell of bread seeps through deep cut stone.
She knows, she knows his flour is ground from bone.

1/4/25
## Why Gen X Can Handle Pretty Much Anything

Jon Bon Jovi wrote "Dead or Alive" in
1986, the same year my friends
placed a rat inside a microwave and
set a 5-minute timer at the local

Fast Fare, some twisted rite of passage for
small town deviants, the same year we watched
the Challenger explode on live TV
73 seconds into its flight,

the same year as the Chernobyl explosion
and meltdown, which spiked already spiked fears,
only three years after *The Day After*
movie about nuclear holocaust.

The same year I wore a skirt too short and
drank too much and trusted the wrong people.

1/5/25
Upskirt


When I tell my kids about movies I loved
in the 80s, I have to be careful,
check first, because I know now how memory
selects. A slew of mommy porn, McFly
edition. Racist sweet 16, *Black Car,*
*Pink Guy*! and don't get me started on Long
Duk Dong, my god, I cringe even thinking
I thought it was funny. Judd Nelson's face
between Ringwald's knees, unwanted opportunist.
She, feeling she had to smile and take it, me,
nodding agreement. That scene, upskirt breach,
vulgar violation for a laugh.


2016. The Fissure. The Rupture.
You're right. I will no longer take a joke.

1/5/25
*Starship Troopers* (the movie)


*Service guarantees citizenship*—cult
classic, first criticized for gore, for its
*bugle-blowing* promotion of fascism.
The enemy? Smart arachnids, brain bug's
mouth unmistakably a vagina,
pulsing, undulating, sticky substance
running from a proboscis able to
suck men's brains, render them useless, lifeless.

The hero? A thick, meaty drill sergeant
who drags brain bug into a circle of
gun-toting men. Later, in a lab,
the "mouth" probed with a long, sharp instrument.

The language of war, always the language
of men. Satire? My ass. Same shit, different time.

1/6/25
Divine

Oh, to be an elephant, massive
pachyderm, their service is to the herd.
Mommas and babies, everyone raises
the silly littles together, communal,
that village Americans ruminate on
but rarely carry through, the idea
of sharing, a *do as I say* situation.

Oh matriarchy! The biggest cow
leads her community through memory,
teaching the others the ways to water.
Proud proboscis, she wields it to greet,
to feed, to spray, to play, to protect.
Oh Mother! You touch and scent the tusks
of your ancestors. May we learn this love again.

1/6/25
# Love and Mourning

My husband kept two girlfriends on the side
working at a zoo: a spider monkey
named Selma who awaited his arrival
every morning, blowing him kisses, and
the other, an elephant named Lady
Bird. When she suddenly died, he catnapped
on her carcass while awaiting the crane
to lift her two-ton body from the dirt.

For over a year, he mourned her, waking
in a cold sweat, nightmaring her death, her
cut-hay smell lingering, haunting his nose.
Her broken tusk imprinted on his skin.

Now a year after his own mother passed,
her belongings rest in boxes still unopened.

1/7/25
Swedish Death Cleanse

Twenty years in my house, longer than
anywhere else I have lived, and there are
boxes and boxes, nostalgia galore,
unopened, imprisoned traditions,
dust-blanketed bins filled with grim
reminders that I am the type to
forget. Object constancy problems
arise the moment I take my eyes off
the item, and then it belongs to the garage
gap, the bleak trunk, the closet hollow,
the vacuity of reusable bags,
the veritable plethora of voids
voluminous. And to my children, I leave
spontaneous combustion instructions.

1/8/25
Daughter's Request Gets Ignored

I only asked for one piece of paper,
name and contact info for creditors
and debtors. I never asked you to
de-clutter, organize your belongings—
the papers and clothes piled in corners—two
things you've always hoarded, stacked and packed in
the perimeters of each room. No, I
only asked for contacts to call upon
your death, accounts to close. But, whatever.
We're combustible, diametrically
opposed. Once, you told me my father may
not be my father. Once, I inked you
into a poem and struck a match. You poked
the ashes as if they never mattered.

1/8/25
How We Compare to the Trees


The glass and metal of my brother's
restoration Camaro had rearranged
themselves, become molten, ebbed and flowed
into installation art resembling
a car. It stood near the carcass of kitchen,
couched in a mountain copse of blackened trees,
their trunks still tall, their California branches
like spokes spiraling, still living witnesses
to the fire's voracious consumption.


As I watch Los Angeles burn, Pacific
Palisades burn where once I sat in envy
of every rich swim kid whose team was better
equipped than ours, we who lived below the
smog line, I am reminded. Money burns.

1/9/25
Bread and Circuses

A California resident looks to
social media to see if and when
she needs to evacuate. Here are photos
from the Golden Globes four days ago;
here's video confirmation the fire
is a cover to burn Diddy evidence;
here are politicos discussing how
to invade Greenland. I scroll late-night TV
and the screen flits between game shows and fire.
*Price is Right* and fire. *Raid the Cage* and fire.
The Palisades Village Starbucks building,
100 years old, stands as charred carcass,
only some arches, a wall of columns left:
the Business Block, American ruins.

1/9/25
How to Invade Greenland

Exploit women. Get lots and lots of women
pregnant. Some won't survive. Have lots and lots
of babies. Some won't survive. Collateral
damage. Exhaust the natural resources
in your immediate area. Learn
there are more natural resources
in lands where you are not. Invade and
colonize. Exploit indigenous peoples.
Some won't survive. Develop technology
to try to reverse the damage you caused.
Learn the resources you need
exist in other countries you can exploit.
Have native peoples dig mines that pollute
pristine lands. Call it jobs. Name yourself savior.

1/9/25
## How to Invade Greenland If That Doesn't Work

Grab her by the land mass, erect a gold
tower on her crevasse, tell the Saudis
and Putin to come, come. Douse the land in
golden showers, take all her wealth, her

people, her power, plow through protestors
and proclaim there's good people on both sides.
Move on her—the deeply troubled countries
are always the best. Just start kissing her.

Claim that you're not invading her. After
all, they just let you do it as long as
you're powerful and wealthy. Nobody
has more respect for Greenland. Nobody.

Nobody has more respect. Oh, Greenland,
you want it. I will be your protector.

1/10/25
## Will the Real McCoy Please Stand Up?

Not long ago, before marriage, women
belonged to their fathers, and after
deemed legally dead, a part of the body
husband. A property, gotten and held.

How is a land grab different from a
handmaid? I'd say something clever,
but the answer is bleak. It's scope,
it's scale, it's a reckoning, a measuring

of dicks. The last thing we need is more
men motivated to own, possession
as law, squatters seeking something for nothing,
a holocaust over notches on a hog's ear.

America the beautiful, feuding,
feudal farce. From sea to stolen sea.

1/10/25
## Mother of Exiles

Lady Liberty, colossal queen bee,

keeper of hive and hearth, contrapposto

pose, skin two-penny thick, sutured copper,

your eyes vacant as an oracle.

Your iron core shifts without cracking.

Only a woman could bear the brunt of

600 lightning strikes and still welcome

the world. Defender of freedom, the chains

lie at your feet. Libertas of the late

republic. Eleutheria of the Greek.

If democracy dies in the daylight,

will your right foot fall, will your torch be doused?

Days, I squat in the spiral of your crown,

see anarchy on the horizon-line.

Note: Poem directly references "The Colossus" by Sylvia Plath

1/10/25
Love Lies Bleeding

In the spiral of your crown,
the smell of crèche, of milk,
miraculous from my breasts,
of bathwater and baby skin,
whorls of the softest down.
You grow into corkscrews
and curlicues, twirling your
dark auburn hair into helixes
housing the tale of your birth.

You are nearly 20 now,
driving your way back to school
in the snow. And I know, I am
selfish. I would welcome you, again
and again, into this wound of a world.

1/10/25
Here We Go Again

*Love lies bleeding*: flowering tendrils, bent
heads with maroon blooms, *amaranthus*
*caudactus*, edible grain, remedy.
A woman on TikTok offers courses
in herbal healing; another in folk
songs whose language is coded instruction
for women—*Let No Man Steal Your Thyme* (rue
will spread). Blue cohosh, mugwort, pennyroyal—
there are many natural tinctures and teas,
ways to cure what ails using root and bark,
secrets passed from mothers on deathbeds to
daughters. Once, kings deployed witchunters to
snuff out women who healed, testing their will
with stones, river water. How little has changed.

1/12/25
## Shu-shu-shu-shu-Schadenfreude

It's time to face the game we are playing,
cameras tracking the reality
of every move, from mini magnetic
nanny cams spying cycles of neglect
and abuse, to elevator and hallway
hotel surveillance making accusations
of unwitnessed celebrity assaults
true, to vehicle real-time dash cams
recording who did what to who and how
it all happened, helpful tools for proof.

But then everyone happily posting
to socials for clicks and likes, monetized
engagement, delusions of grandeur by
proxy of pain. We revel in it. We riot.

1/12/25
Perp Walk

Scene: stage center, mid-morning, December:
a shackled and handcuffed man in orange
jumpsuit, head bowed, surrounded by 18
men, some wearing ties, others wearing
uniforms, men in foreground with full
military gear—black combat helmets,
bulletproof vests, armed to the teeth with guns,
automatic rifles, ammo. Lower
Manhattan skyline ghosted in the back.

Dramatic spectacle, choreographed
for the court of public opinion,
innocence never presumed, just denied.
Whether we revel or riot, it's hard
to identify who's villain or hero.

1/13/25
## Green Mario

My kids will forever ridicule me
for not knowing Mario had a brother,
younger and shy. I was tired in the Wal-Mart,
buying underwear again for kids who
kept growing and needing new, plus I had
already worked a full day teaching numbers
2,000 - 2,200,
students at my university job
that didn't pay me enough to buy
new underwear for my kids much less leave
their father who would give his eye teeth
to do nothing forever, the farthest
from Luigi, renowned warrior,
that you can get. Am I really expected
to believe that this kid, not much older
than my own, masterminded a hit
in the midst of a busy city street but
showed his face to flirt with a barista?
Got caught at McDonalds just sitting there,
eating his hashbrown? When is the last time
you actually sat in McDonalds? But
anyways, it's as believable as
Beethoven's 5th killing cancer cells
Da da da dum, da da da dum, da da
-ism for fuck's sake which pill did we take?
Luigi is derived from Ludwig,
famous in battle: multiplayer
mode. Together, we can do anything.

1/14/25
# When I Reach the Place I'm Going

So many grasp at straws. So many need
something to believe in. Trust me. I get it.
I was born pitchfork-angry, ready to
rage. I understand gunning it through red
lights, screaming into the void, storming
capitals—spit-face-fury in my blood.
My great grandfather was chained to a tree
with the family dog because his mother
died and his father had to work the line.
My other greats changed their names to sound more
*American*—Luigi became Lewis,
Gandolfo became Randolph. I understand
scraping and scrapping because I've had to
forever, each day treading water in
the same retention pond, each night awake
worrying. Together, we can do
anything—anything is possible.
We've been force-fed platitudes our whole lives.
So, who's to say it's impossible that
various vibrations kill cancer cells?
That aliens are coming to invade
New Jersey? That Covid came from cell phones?
That we live in a simulation and
an adrenochrome-drinking cabal
controls all? That we share false memories?
I know what I saw with my own eyes:
Cobain wore a pink feathery jacket;
the bears were spelled Berenstein all along.

1/14/25
A Denial

Maybe, if the Monopoly Man
wore a monocle like we remember,
like he's supposed to, like the *hmmm...*
emoji we send when we think something's
wonky, something's wibbly wobbly,
something's not quite right, then maybe
Kurt Cobain didn't kill himself and
he wore a pink feathery jacket
with wide white Elton John glasses
and all is right with this version
of the world, and questions are answered
before we close the book and turn off the light.

I tell you, I remember being in love.
And the DJ played "Smells Like Teen Spirit."

1/15/25
How the Game is Played

In 1906, Lizzie Magie placed
an ad in the paper: herself, for sale:
"young woman American slave," it read,
daring the public to contend with the dire
financial prospects of women. She once
penned a short story about a therapist
plagiarizing a hypnotized patient's
novel. She also invented the first
iteration of Monopoly. But
Charles Darrow, an unemployed salesman, claimed
the game his, made millions, credited as
its inventor until the 1970s.

There are official rules to every game.
Half the population ignores them.

1/16/25
Whisper Network

So many women made monsters.
In myth, Medusa turned men to stone,
never again able to gaze into
a lover's eyes, serpentine punishment
for her own rape. Rapist in the form of
a swan, a shower of gold, a holy
possession, conception, virgin birth.

So many women lower their voices,
whisper their warnings of monstrous men.
This one will flirt with you, flatter you, force
you through threat via power dynamics,
deliver gods-level gaslighting,
official rules, non-disclosure agreements.
Flash ghoulish grins and claim to be sheep.

1/16/25
## Girl's Guide to Monstrous Men

Be gracious. Be nice. Smile. Avoid hurting
someone's feelings. You're probably imagining
it anyway. Ignore the catcalls. Keep
walking. Carry your keys between your fingers.

Do not walk alone at night. Do not walk
in alleyways. Go out in groups. Watch behind
your back. Watch the periphery. Watch what
everyone is doing. Be modest. Don't

wear skimpy clothes. Don't drink. Hold your drink
and keep it covered. Look under your car.
Look in your backseat. Memorize the exits.
Make sure someone always knows where you're at.

Go for the eyes first. Act crazy. (See hysterical.) Vomit.
Be good. Bad things don't happen to good girls.

1/17/25
Not All Who Wander

Not their eyes, not their hands, but our flesh,

discrete piece, seat of sex. The "hysteria"

experienced by women explained away

by location of womb in the *Malleus*

*Maleficarum*, women as witches

bound to hammer out their lives in hovels

stained in herbal remedy and menstrual

blood, desperate for semen, soul searchers

seeking solutions for sadness, seminal

cures for depression, strapped down in rooms,

remanded to uterus. Reminder:

ritual ripping of wallpaper is


cause for committal. I am beyond

belabored mollification. Let's bare our teeth.

1/18/25
Menagerie

Standing in my backyard, surveying
the landscape: where once were thick woods, birdsong,
family of deer, now a vinyl-sided
apartment complex. Black birds fly in V
over a slate sky. Something magical
happens at 50 or so, fully brewed
confidence, a no-giving-a-fuck-ness,
the no-longer blood, that monthly auger,
the no-longer drill and shed of yourself,
realizing that love is a choice you make
and not something that happens to you.
The male god wanted us punished. Now,

land barren, the remaining owls hoot from
a lone tree. I worry for our daughters.

1/18/25
Step Right Up


The remaining owls are worried.

Force fed rodents, allowed no autonomy

in which to digest the soft parts, skin

and innards, they regurgitate words

that would hurt them, tooth and claw, in compact

packages on chamber floors, exposed enclosures.


Trapped behind bullet-proof glass, we watch blackbirds

murmurate, gather on barren landscapes.

This all means something. On display in our

offices, we are told we are complex

domestics. We collect pellets behind

electric fences. Secretly slice them open.


While the barker is busy hoodwinking

the horde, we hatch plans. We throw bones.

1/19/25
## Manifest

Pitch, save for the library's lights
on a distant hill. The starlings are still
again. On the kitchen table a Five
of Cups, Ten of Swords, the Tower, the Fool.

Someone somewhere watches *Wheel of Fortune*
in their darkened den. Someone asks Siri
to play "O Fortuna!" as she butchers
a bird, severs sternum from pectoral girdle.

Long ago, ladies of the lake were summoned
to test the bravery and virtue of men.
In one version of the story, a lesson:
those who promise to protect often take your head.

*Sors immanis, Et inanis, Rota*
*tu volubilis.* We wait for morning.

1/19/25
## Wheel in the Sky

I know exactly where I'll be tomorrow,

right here, keeping house, foolish foot on the edge

of a precipice men manufactured

for me so long ago I've forgotten

the monstrous apocryphal fate

of it all. Barring death, of course, I will

be here, begetting the fruits of the spin cycle.

Ezekiel's wheels within wheels breeding

theories, ancient astronauts, drones hover

over the eastern seaboard, gyroscopes

and perpetual motion machines empty

but still whirling. Perhaps men are tempted

because they have a death wish, a tendency

to end things. Women, begin. Grip your swords.

1/19/25
*Pernicious Hour*

*Tomorrow, and tomorrow, and tomorrow*
an unjust king promoted unjustly,
apocryphal transfer cloaked in darkness.
Fulcrum of freedom, measure
of load and effort, imbalance, unhinged,
unstable, dis-ease multiplying
in the body politic, malignant
spread to marrow, radiating.
Carnival freak, barker, snake oil salesman,
overnight crypto billionaire, still
*an idiot, full of sound and fury.*
We march, gather, form secret circles, wield
swords, intuition spike-sharp, premonition,
we warned: *something wicked this way comes.*

Note: Italicized lines from Shakespeare's *Macbeth*

# Acknowledgments

Thanks to the editors of these journals for first publishing these poems:

*South Florida Poetry Journal*, May 2025 issue:
    "How We Compare to the Trees"
    "Bread and Circuses"
    "How to Invade Greenland"
    "How to Invade Greenland if That Doesn't Work"

*BRILLIG: a micro-lit mag*, Spring 2025
    "#tradwife"
    "Revealing"
    "Abscess"
    "Plunder"

*Blood+Honey*, October 24, 2025
    "Strange Beast"
    "Surviving Fallout"
    "Realignment"
    "New Year, New Outlook"
    "Ignition"

Kathleen Nalley is the author of the prose poetry collection, *Gutterflower* (winner of the Bryant-Lisembee Editor's Prize), as well as the poetry chapbooks *Nesting Do.* (winner of the S.C. Poetry Initiative Prize) and *American Sycamore*. Her poetry and book reviews have appeared in *New Flash Fiction Review*, *Slipstream*, *Limp Wrist*, *Southern Humanities Review*, *The Bitter Southerner*, *storySouth*, and elsewhere, and her poetry has been anthologized in several collections.


Gabrielle Brant Freeman's award winning and Pushcart nominated poetry has been published in many journals, including *Barrelhouse*, *The Rumpus*, *One*, *Scoundrel Time*, and *storySouth*. Press 53 published her book, *When She Was Bad*. In 2021, Gabrielle's poetry was included in the collaborative creation of the choreopoem, *A Chorus Within Her*, performed at Theater Alliance in Washington, DC. She lives in Eastern North Carolina with her family.

# About Small Harbor Publishing

Small Harbor Publishing is a 501c3 nonprofit organization. Our goal is to publish unique and diverse voices. We are a feminist press, and we are committed to diversity and inclusion. We strive to bring new voices to a devoted and expanding readership.

Small Harbor Publishing began in 2018 with the first issue of *Harbor Review*. The magazine is an online space where poetry and art converse. *Harbor Review* quickly grew and now publishes reviews and runs multiple micro chapbook competitions, including the Washburn Prize and the Editor's Prize.

In July 2020, Small Harbor Publishing was officially incorporated and began Harbor Editions. Harbor Editions accepts submissions through a chapbook open reading period, a hybrid chapbook open reading period, the Marginalia Series, and the Laureate Prize.

In 2023, Harbor Anthologies began with a mission to promote texts that explore social justice issues and highlight marginalized writers.

If you would like to support Small Harbor Publishing, visit our "About" page at: smallharborpublishing.com/about.

www.ingramcontent.com/pod-product-compliance
Lightning Source LLC
Chambersburg PA
CBHW020215090426
42734CB00008B/1083